Pedro 'n' Pip

By
Taylor Barton

A Rock 'n' Roll Odyssey

ISBN number 978-1-48357-412-7
© Taylor Barton, 2016 Library of Congress
© Music and lyrics, Surewill Music, Ascap

Acknowledgements

I wish to thank so many people who helped me finish this journey.
First and foremost, GE Smith, Paul Ossola, Jeff Kazee, Tony Shanahan,
Alex Alexander and Shawn Pelton who brought my melodies to life.
My kind friends who donated their talents early on, Christine Ohlman,
Bruce Henderson, and my good friend who is no longer with us, Rebecca Dorsey.

Those who backed my kickstarter campaign: Wilson Ervin, Maggie Hadleigh-West,
April Gornik, Cassis Staudt, Lynn Evans, Chub Whitten, Andrea Sacker-Klein.
A big hearty love and appreciation to those who recorded the score, James Frazee,
Cynthia Daniels, and Steve Addabbo.
Most heartfelt thanks to Patricia Birch my lifelong mentor, director and inspiration.
And lastly my dearest friend who hung in there in my darkest hour, Dana Cooper.

Dedicated to my mother, Meta Packard Barton

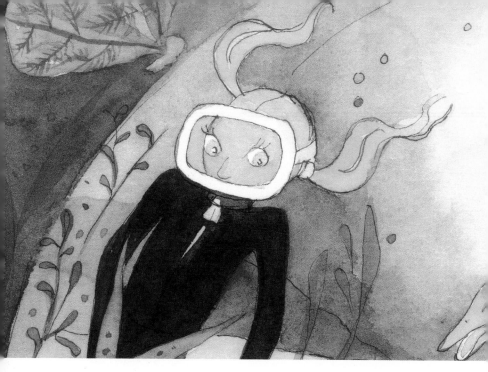

CONTENTS

"Don't Quit"	performed by Taylor Barton
"Pedro 'n' Pip's Rap"	performed by Ella Moffly, Robbie Wyckoff
"Everybody Knows"	performed by Robbie Wyckoff

PART IV   OCEAN DAY

Songs:

"Eight-Chord Star (Reprise)"	performed by Robbie Wyckoff
"Move Me"	performed by Robbie Wyckoff, Christine Ohlman
"Eight-Chord Star"	performed by Robbie Wyckoff

Recording: James Frazee, Hobo Sound, Weehawken, NJ
The Band: GE Smith, (guitars) Jeff Kazee, (B3 Hammond) Tony Shanahan (bass) Alex Alexander (djembe and drums)
Additional Recording: Steve Addabbo, Shelter Sound, NYC
Recording, Mixed and Mastered by Cynthia Daniels, Monk Music, East Hampton, NY
Art: © Dana Cooper Designs, 2016

For Music & Audio
http://www.cdbaby.com/cd/taylorbarton13

Part 1
The Newsflash

It was a sunny, hot day in October. In fact, the fall in New Orleans remained warm until November. Pip, a jubilant nine-year-old, and her dog, Seaweed, were cleaning up after a vigorous round of fetch and agility training. Her mom was watering her cactus garden. Pip was singing a little tune, and Seaweed added harmony—by yelping.

THE FIRST WORD GO

I like the birds, and I like the trees.
I don't even mind the stinging of the bees.
I like sunsets, and I like lagoons.
I often try listening to the voices of the moon.

I like to swim, and I like to play ball
But my parents are always afraid I'm going to fall.
I always say yes, the world says no,
I know I can win, from the first word go
I know I can win, from the first word go.

"That-a-boy, Seaweed. Treat?" Pip tossed Seaweed a bone, and practicing the Spanish that she had learned at school, she said, "Aquí. Seaweed, aquí!" The dog cocked its ears and followed her command and retrieved the bone. "Ahora…now, bring it to your master!" Seaweed ignored her and gnawed on his bone. "You're just like ragweed, difficult."

Pip's mother brushed sweat from her head. "We're almost finished, Pip. Once our ground is tilled we can plant our petunias."

"Can't we take a day off?" Pip whined. I want to set the table for my dog party!"

Her mother smiled. "You're right. You will be ten soon, and that's reason to celebrate. You're almost a woman."

"I don't to be a woman; I'm still a kid. I want to stay young forever." Pip stalked off, and Seaweed trailed right behind.

Her mother furrowed her brows. "What on earth has gotten into you, Pip? Growing up is the best part of childhood."

Pip screamed, "I don't want to lose my imaginary friends! They make me feel safe."

Seaweed was compassionate and agreed by dog-talking. "Ruff, Right!"

"Did you hear that, Mom?" Seaweed spoke.

Her mother said, "I think you will like being a tween, sweetheart. Can you please put Seaweed's hurdles away? Remember, dear, 'Actions speak louder than words.'"

Pip yawned and told her mom she wanted to watch *The Dog Whisperer.*

Her mom kissed her dirty forehead, and shrugged "OK."

Pip dashed into the house. After getting a glass of lemonade, Pip and Seaweed were plopped down in front of the TV when T*he Dog Whisperer* was interrupted by a newsflash.

"A catastrophic collision has caused another oil spill in the Gulf of Mexico. These animals and fish are dependent on our ability to maintain a clean sea. You can help by sending donations to: P.O. Box 800, Houston, Texas or call 1-800-SEA-HELP."

Tears welled up when Pip saw the dying dolphins on the flat screen. The idea of those poor sea creatures drowning in oil was unbearable. She cried as she watched filthy seagulls and oil-slicked birds struggling to get ashore, and she softly sang.

THE FIRST WORD GO (REPRISE)

I have a dream to make this world clean,
Like the feathers of ducks or the glistening seas.
I'll jump in the ocean and cause a commotion
With the underwater creatures, they're my favorite preachers.

I always say yes—the world says no
But I know I can win from the first word go.

Pip was determined to respond to the creatures in need. She would bring the problem up at dinner when her father, an oil trader, returned from work. She knew her father would be tired, so her approach had to be very clever.

That evening, Pip took special care setting the table. She encouraged her mom to make fried chicken, her favorite dish. She even offered to wash the lettuce. "Mom, what's it like to be old?"

"Well, there are lots of responsibilities. People have to take care of their homes, cook, clean. Why do you ask, Pip?" She was unaccustomed to Pip's assistance in the kitchen.

"Oh, it's just that I saw something totally awful on TV! Dying dolphins."

Pip's mom said, "Oh, the oil spill. Your father is in a huff about that!"

Pip asked her mother why her father worked in a place that killed dolphins and birds. Her mother assured her that the newsflash was about an accident, not something that happened at Saxton Oil her father's company. She said, "Two tankers collided off the Gulf. Dad did not do that!"

Pip said, "Well, I want to save those dying creatures." She told her mom how the newscaster said volunteers were needed to clean up the spill and that there might be a prize given to those who helped the most. Pip said, "I love dolphins. I want to get that ugly black oil off their backs! Seaweed can help find the floundering birds on shore."

Her mom said, "We'll see" and reminded Pip that her friends were coming tomorrow at five for her dog party. "I've made bones with chocolate icing, and, remember, be extra careful in the yard. No roughhousing!"

"Are you a moron, Mom? Dogs can't eat chocolate!"

Pip asked four friends and their pups to a special canine carnival. A trainer was going to come and teach K-9 basic search and rescue skills. Then they would have a scavenger hunt, and after that, a potato-sack race led by the pups.

Pip's mom asked, "what kind of dogs were attending?"

"There will be an Irish Wolfhound, a Lab, a Dalmatian, and a Chihuahua."

Pip's mother said, "Those pups must wait outside when we have pizza. I don't want them pooping and peeing all over my living room."

"Mom, I forgot to ask you for something that I really need?"

"I got you everything on your list, case closed."

"But I need a mask, a regulator, a wet suit, and scuba diving gear!"

Her mother's eyebrows knotted. She dismissed Pip's plea. "Where is your father? He's always late!" They sat down and started without him.

"Pip?"

Pip offered the prayer. "Grace on the table, grace on the wall, for God's sake's, Grace, don't eat it all."

Finally, Pip's father arrived during chocolate pudding. He had the paper. The headlines read: "Hot Seat for Saxton Oil! Catastrophic Collision."

"Where's my kiss," her father bellowed. "I've had a day in purgatory."

After an abnormal amount of silence, Pip asked, "Why, Dad? Are you in trouble? Are you going to get fired?"

Her mother looked horrified and said, "Of course not!"

Her father said blankly, "It's not that big of a deal!"

Her mom said gently, "could you get fired?"

Pip's father was abrupt and shouted his favorite military term: "Stand clear, and get that mutt out of here!"

Pip obeyed and ushered Seaweed outside. Pip's father said he was not going to get fired. "I only made the transaction with the barge. I am not personally responsible for the collision."

Pip returned to the table when it occurred to her that her classmates, who were coming to her party, might make fun of her or her father. She had just given a report on oil tankers in her public-speaking class. Her classmates were impressed by her speech and were looking forward to meeting her dad.

Pip thought that this might be a good opportunity to advise her father to help clean up the spill. "Hey, Dad, can't we do something totally awesome, like help? Yo tengo ayude?"

"Speak English, girl! This is New Orleans, not Tijuana!"

Her mother whispered, "She's learning Spanish, and her Girl Scout troop is helping the Hispanics who are new to our city."

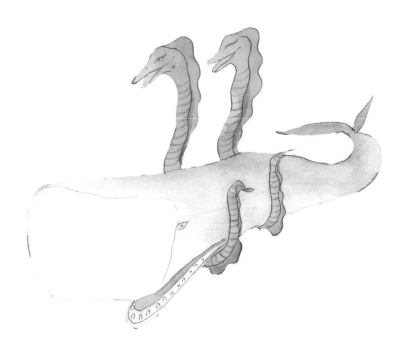

13

Her father buried himself in his paper. "Let's eat!"

Pip had an idea. "Dad, we should try something new, like scuba diving. We could really aid in the cleanup."

"Scuba diving?"

"We could rescue dolphins and whales, maybe win the prize, and save your job."

Pip's mother thought the idea was good. "Besides," she said sweetly to her husband, "you might lose some weight."

He reluctantly suggested they learn tennis or croquet, preferably something on land.

Her mother recited a homily: "Remember, Pip, competition is victory in itself!" Then, out of frustration, she yelled at Pip's father. "You only think about yourself. Do you know what tomorrow is?"

Pip was persistent. "Dad, I want to try scuba. Please, Dad, don't you know what tomorrow is?"

Her father looked baffled and said, "Our anniversary?"

Pip's Mom hissed, "That was last week, honey. It's Pip's pooch party!"

Pip felt rejected and wandered into the den to watch TV. The sea creatures were still disoriented, dying, and homeless. There was an underwater interview with a scuba diver, newscaster, and three singing sea creatures. The sea creatures identified themselves as Juan, a boisterous eel; Consuelo, a sexy starfish; and Wally the Whale, a limousine chauffeur. The scuba diver asked, "How has the oil spill affected your lives?" A song was their answer.

THE KINGDOM FROM KYO

We stopped sleeping when they dumped the first can
Of oil and trash all over our land.
Mankind never considered their blow.
They wiped out our believers in one large throw.
Now we're homeless, some dead, some alive.
We're trying to live, but it's hard to survive.

The newscaster interrupted the song and said, "These sea creatures need your input. The starfish Consuelo sang her solo. She was a sweet, little thing with an angelic voice.

Our heavenly host gave us this earth
To breathe and create in constant rebirth.
Beautiful skies and valleys below,
I spend my days resisting the foe.
I'm so in awe of the love that you sow,
I'll always protect our Kingdom from Kyo.

Wally the Whale explained that "Kyo" is the Japanese word for depletion of energy. He said, "I learned that word from a blowfish who drifted all the way from Japan."

Consuelo winked at the underwater camera, and Juan wrapped himself around Wally's spout. They harmonized.

Dear God, please tell me there is something to do.
We're givin' up trying from feelin' so blue.
Our efforts were useless in this lifetime plan,
And now it's time to start living again.
We're counting on you to see us through,
We're your vessels here and our channels are clear.

Wally the Whale whispered, "Remember, we're in a state of Kyo!"

The newscaster reminded Pip that every effort counts.

Pip ran out screaming at her father to google 'Sea-Help'. "I want to scuba, Dad. I have to!"

Pip's Dad said, "We'll discuss it in the morning!" That was his way of saying, "no."

That evening Pip's parents were lying in bed, heavy in discussion. Her mom said, "Honey, why are you so irate?"

"I'm in so much hot water. I'll be lucky if I still have a job tomorrow."

"Well, if your reputation at work is at stake, you need to do something proactive."

"Like what? The damage is done."

"Something hands-on." She was mad at him for ignoring Pip's ideas.

He said, "Don't pester me about that. You know I'm petrified of the ocean. If there were millions of people in the ocean,

Jaws would find me!"

She said, "Please, for Pip's sake. Can't you reconsider scuba diving? Take a risk. Sometimes walking through fear eliminates it. Be courageous. How can you be afraid of *Jaws*? It's pure fiction. Be a role model for Pip, and show her when things go wrong, you get to work. It would make Pip so happy!"

Pip's father softened, as the words soothed his soul. He said, "OK, maybe I'll like it."

After kissing him on the cheek, she said, "Don't quit."

The following morning Pip's father was a half hour early for work. He knew that his boss, Morty, would blame him for the spill because he was responsible, even though he couldn't have prevented the accident. He brokered the transaction of the two tankers. In Morty's eyes, that would make him the "fall guy." He entered the high-rise, repeating his wife's mantra, "Don't quit, don't quit!"

The moment he stepped in his office, Mary, Morty's secretary, informed him that Morty wanted to see him. "Pronto, Mr. Sampson!"

As he entered the office, Morty was leaning back in a red leather armchair, smoking a fat cigar. He blasted Pip's father with the following accusation: "Peter, it has come to my attention that you were responsible for the barge that collided with the tanker in the Gulf. Now we got everyone from the fishermen in the swamplands to the shrimpers in Alabama screaming bloody murder. The governor is coming down on us, and we need to run damage control."

Morty instructed him to call a press conference on the firm's behalf and to announce that the company would supply monetary support for a cleanup. "That means a cut in your salary and no bonus. Comprendo?"

"Why certainly, Morty. I've even considered taking scuba diving lessons, so I can personally assist in the manual cleanup!"

Morty said, "I'm impressed. I personally would not even

consider going near the Gulf because it's a cesspool." He wished him the best of luck. "That's all! Dismissed." Pip's father tripped over his own feet because he could barely breathe from Morty's cigar smoke.

On his way back to his office, Mary offered him his daily doughnut. He reluctantly declined. "I've got to lose weight."

Pip's father was heard over the intercom instructing Mary to call the morning *Sentinel* and schedule a press conference. And then he said, "Also phone the local Y."

Mary lifted an eyebrow and said, "The Y?"

Pip's father moaned and said, "Please sign my daughter and me up for scuba lessons." And he whined, "No questions!" Mary silently wrote down his instructions and dialed the YMCA.

A week later Pip and her Dad pulled into the Y. Lots of people were piling out of cars with scuba gear, walking awkwardly toward the building, weighted down by the snorkels and flippers.

Pip was ecstatic. She was skipping toward the entrance with Seaweed in tow, chattering to her dad. "We'll see the coolest starfish and bluefish, and maybe some eels and barracudas." Remembering Wally, the singing mammal, she said, "If we're lucky, we can ride a whale! Dad, isn't it sad that those dolphins are dying with oil all over them?"

Her father was irritated and said, "How many times do I have to tell you that the spill did not happen in my department...It was a mistake!"

Pip hid her excitement and said, "Well, we're gonna clean up the spill!"

Her dad asked another overweight man, where the darn pool was?

They entered a room with an Olympic-sized pool. A lean lifeguard was seated at a desk, signing in people.

Pip ran ahead, screaming, "Here, Dad, here!" Seaweed started barking enthusiastically.

Pip's father yelled, "Pipe down." He approached the lifeguard and said, "How much, how long, and whatever!"

The lifeguard, sized up Pip's father, dog and Pip and said, "Six Mondays for one hundred dollars, and an extra fifty for the dog, and seventy-five for a final certification that will be given if you pass the test in the pool."

Pip's father didn't listen to details, just said, "Fine...where do I sign?"

Pip assembled the flippers, wet suits, and masks, and said, "Cool!"

The lifeguard instructed everyone to get in the pool and begin breathing. "Use your snorkels like an oxygen mask!" It was an exercise to demonstrate how to work a regulator, the device used while scuba diving.

Pip's father spat into his mask, but it was too tight. "My God, I haven't gained that much weight."

"Mom said seventeen pounds!" Everyone in the pool chuckled, especially the lifeguard, and her father was annoyed. He lost grip of his snorkel, and it sank right to the bottom of the pool. Seaweed, the hero, jumped in and fetched the sunken snorkel.

Pip and her dad attended all six lessons faithfully. They learned the buddy system, which involved both Pip and her dad breathing off the same regulator.

Her father said, "We will never get separated underwater. Seaweed will make sure of that!" Seaweed was circling them constantly, herding them toward the steps of the pool.

Pip exclaimed, "That's for sure. Seaweed was top dog and took first place at my dog party for his rescue skills! We're buddies, right?"

Pip's father said, "Certifiable."

On the last Monday, Pip passed the scuba test with flying colors. Her father barely passed, but both graduated. Seaweed was awarded a blue ribbon for water rescue. The lifeguard sang at the ceremony while handing out the diplomas.

CERFTIFICATION SONG

You have spent several weeks,
You're performing at your peak,
These parting words I speak:
Stay safe and watch for leaks.

Look for light under the land
With a joy for other men.
Stay close, stay hand in hand.
You're welcome on the land.

If you have a question, call.
I'll be back to teach next fall.
I hope you've enjoyed it all.
You can sign up at the mall.

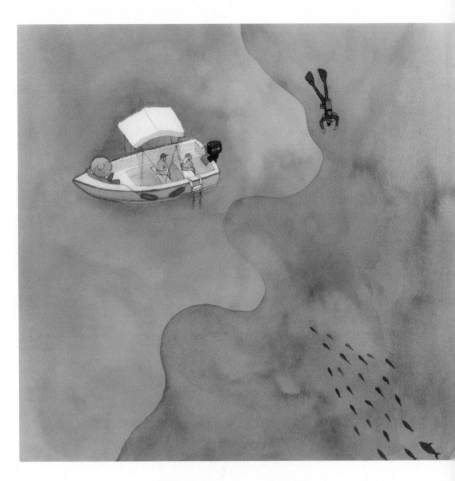

Part 11
Scuba Diving

A month went by. No scuba diving yet. Pip's father was stalling because he was still afraid of the ocean. "Sweetie, maybe we can go next year. I have to save for the trip."

Her father felt safe in a pool, but not the ocean where there were sharks. Furthermore, there was mounting trouble at Saxton Oil. The company was under legal scrutiny by the federal government, and litigation was underway.

Her father was working long hours, sometimes arriving home after Pip's bedtime. But Pip was persistent. "Come on, Dad. I want to scuba, Sea-Help needs our hands. Let's do it."

Pip's mom was getting nasty looks from her friends at the women's club. For some reason, the women found it easier to blame her for the oil spill. "Mrs. Sampson," said a noisy, chatterbox, "your husband's in a lot of hot water, isn't he?"

She responded tersely, "I believe it's none of your beeswax."

After what seemed like an eternity, Pip's father finally made plans. "Sweetie, look what I got here—two tickets to Mexico. What do you say? I bought a scuba weekend deal to Cozumel."

"Is it on the Gulf, Dad? If it is, we can get started on the cleanup. Right dad? Why are we going all the way to Mexico?"

"The water is cleaner."

"We'll see all those eels and barracudas," she said.

Pip's mom packed a knapsack filled with light clothing. Pip included her trusty miner flashlight that her mom had given her as a going-away present. She pecked Pip on the forehead and said, "Remember, Pip, don't quit!"

Pip ran ahead of her father and said, "I love you, Mom. Don't forget to play fetch with Seaweed, and you need to run him on the tracking course daily."

After a two-hour plane ride, Pip and her father had cleared customs and arrived at El Presidente, a hotel with a right on the beach. All the locals had been extremely helpfu from the moment they arrived. The customs guys waved th through, and the cab drivers were friendly and cordial.

"This way, turistas," said a man who wore a straw ha a wide brim. "You need a ride?"

"Certainly," said a self-assured Pip.

He tilted his sombrero and smiled, while hoisting t

gear in the trunk. He had gleaming, pearly white teeth.

They had to wait until the evening to check into the hotel because the maids were running a little late with their cleaning. "Sorry, chiquita, una problema."

Pip convinced her irate father, who looked disheveled after the plane ride, to change into their bathing suits in a straw-thatched cabana, which was adjacent to the pool. Guests were drinking piña coladas, and floating on rafts, taking in the sun.

Her father emerged from the cabana in some really expensive scuba gear, and Pip said, "Check it out, Dad. Palm trees and pelicans," as she picked up the equipment that her dad kept dropping.

They approached a wooden shack that had a sign that read "scuba." It was obvious to everyone that Pip and her dad were novices. Two scruffy men, Señors Jaime and Cucho, the operators of the establishment, were also instructors who looked like gangsters. Jaime had gold teeth and Cucho was unshaven with a scar across his cheek.

Cucho said, "passaporte?" Then he broke into a song.

PASSAPORTE REQUIRED

CHORUS
By the cabana, we offer three rules:
You pay us first, don't get sunburned,
And passaporte required.

(Jaime)

You take the scuba gear and place your face in here,
And breathe a little air.
You let your hair fall 'round, as you glide right down
The dark and watery town.
And when a fish swims by, let out a scary sigh,
But trust your mighty leader.
You hold your buddy's hand, until you reach the land.
That's what we call the skin diver.

CHORUS

When the day comes 'round, you settle down
At the fiesta by the pool.
We serve tropical drinks to señoritas in pink
Enchiladas to follow.
So sign your name right here, we'll take care of the gear
And have a wonderful time.
And if you want to sign on the dotted line
We can take you fishing mañana.

CHORUS
(Jaime and Cucho)

By the cabana, we offer three rules:
You pay us first, don't get sunburned,
And passaporte required.

"¡Hola!" Jaime said cheerfully.

Then they both said, "¿Dígame? Windsurfing, scuba, fishing, parasailing, waterskiing, jet ski, snorkeling. ¿Dígame?"

Pip, a wiz in Spanish, said that "hola" means "hello." Dígame means "Tell me," and then her father asked Cucho if he could take them scuba diving. He informed the instructors that they would like to see some fish.

"And reefs and eels," squealed Pip.

Jaime smiled, revealing his gold front tooth and said, "Bueno." That means "good." He introduced himself and said, "This is Cucho!"

"Hey, Dad, remember what the lifeguard said? Prices are competitive so talk the men down." This was the third time Pip had recited this information to her father.

Pip's father decided to do a little bargaining. He put on a straight face and said, "How much?"

Cucho said, "A hundred dólares."

"Dólares! It says pesos on the sign!"

Jaime said, "My mistake," and Cucho added, "Dólares, amigo."

Her father said, "Watch this, Pip. Pay attention because this is how you can drive the price down. Fifty dólares, take it or leave it."

Jaime said, "Fifty for the girlie," and Cucho said, "One hundred for the fat boy," and Jaime closed with "A hundred and fifty dólares altogether."

Pip's father screamed, "What?"

Jaime and Cucho mimicked Pip's father and said, "Bargain price!" They broke out in laughter.

They boarded a white fishing boat, and Jaime tooted a little horn that rose above the hull. It signaled to the señoritas that they were leaving. The ladies gathered at the shore and waved. Pip, her dad, and the instructors traveled ten minutes out to sea, when Cucho cut the engine. While throwing an anchor overboard, he said, "We're here!"

Jaime and Pip quickly put on their masks, regulators, flashlights, flippers, and weight belts. Pip's father procrastinated with Cucho.

Jaime and Pip jumped overboard. Pip said, "Sweet!"

Pip's petrified father clung to the railing. "How deep is this? Not more then ten feet you said."

"You a coward, gringo? It is at least forty feet. Now get off the boat." They both fell overboard with a large splash.

The ocean seemed very clear when on the boat, but once they were in it, the water appeared to be much darker. They descended slowly to adjust to the depth comfortably.

The first thing Pip saw was a large turtle, which was freckled with orange spots, gliding to her left.

Meanwhile, Jaime was pointing at debris, mouthing, "Pollution," and Pip's father thought, its not from our oil spill. The turtle's gills waved softly back and forth when suddenly a starfish appeared. She had beautiful eyes and lovely little tentacles. She looked so cute dancing beside the turtle. She yodeled, and Pip said, "Hey, you look familiar. You were on TV!"

The starfish said, "Sí. ¡Mi nombre es Consuelo!"

Cucho told Pip to tell the starfish her name.

"My name is Pip. I'm here to clean up your ocean."

Consuelo said, "Gracias. Follow me; I'll introduce you to some of my friends. We've been waiting for you."

Jaime signaled to Pip and her father to descend deeper. They were following Consuelo's trail. She left sweet, little air bubbles as markers. All sorts of things flushed from the sea bottom—big algae eaters, minnows, and round blowfish. Pip touched what she thought was a barnacle, but it turned out to be a porcupine fish, and it darted to the right.

Pip's father was warning Pip about a reef when suddenly he screamed, "Watch out for that barracuda!"

He scurried away but went up instead of down. Cucho followed him and they resurfaced near their boat. Pip's father said, "Holy Moly, I'm not really the diving type. Let's get out."

Cucho said, "You're like a cocktail to him. He's only interested in protein. You're all blubber."

"Where's my daughter?"

"Jaime will take good care of her. ¿Cerveza?"

"Oh, I love beer. In fact, I'd love one now."

They climbed aboard the boat and Cucho said, "You sissy. Your daughter's much braver than you!"

Feeling his masculinity was being threatened, Pip's father said, "I beg your pardon. I am the client."

Cucho said, "OK, gringo. I was only kidding."

Concurrently, Jaime and Pip were still descending. The sea had gotten very dark, so Jaime flipped on his headlight. Consuelo led them into a little sea cave.

Pip's flashlight spotted a family of eels who dispersed as her light hit the nest. Consuelo introduced the slithering snakes. She said, "Yo, this is Juan. He's kind of real protective. He's like a chief bodyguard. He's the toughest snake in town. He's toothless from eating his conquests."

Jaime remained very still, while Juan wrapped himself around Pip.

Pip got a little scared and looked to Jaime for help. Unaware of what to do, she blurted out, "I know you!"

Juan said, "You do?" He eased his grip and circled around her. Juan sensed her apprehension and said, "We're just as nervous as you."

Pip, relieved of her fear, said, "Yes, you were crying for help on TV."

Juan said, "Did you hear that, boys! We were on TV." The other eels remained indifferent. "We're famous!"

Consuelo lifted a questioning eye and bellowed, "Not as

famous as my man, Pedro. Pip. Pedro is a reclusive rocktopus, and he hasn't sung in years."

Juan said, "Pedro says we're all a bunch of deadbeats, nothing but slime."

Consuelo poked Juan with her star steeple. "That's a wrap, Juan. Pip, you have a request?"

Pip looked around for her father, and Jaime pointed toward the surface of the sea. Pip shrugged and summoned up her courage. She said, "Well, Juan, I'm Pip, and I want to help clean up your home." She noticed that without sunlight, the ocean was colorless. "With cleaner water, you will have a brighter future. More kids will come scuba diving if the water was clean. We love playing with things in the sea."

Suddenly, Juan noticed Jaime. "Who the heck, are you?" he demanded.

Jaime was speechless and gurgled, "Nobody. I'm nobody."

"Take it easy, Juan. He's my guide." Pip moved closer to Juan. "Can I touch you?"

"Most certainly not!" Juan ordered the eels: "Listen up, boys. We've got potential prowlers." The eels got frightened, bumped into each other, and got all entangled.

Consuelo interrupted the eels. "Knock it off, knuckleheads. You're supposed to be guarding the entrance to Pedro's quarters."

"Oh brother," said Juan. "Consuelo, could you please untangle us?" He whispered to Pip, "I'm the boss of these morons."

Consuelo yodeled to her groupies and used the ends of her stars to undo the knots. "Girls, get your slap happy butts over here. The boys are in a maze."

Just then, Pip and Jaime decided to ascend, but got separated in the process because Jaime had turned off his headlights.

"Jaime, Jaime, are your there? Consuelo, Juan, anybody?" Pip was still in the cave. She sat herself down on a rock ridge. "I guess I'll just wait for someone to find me." She was beginning to feel lost, so she calmed herself by singing her favorite tune.

I always say yes; the world says no.
But I know I can win
from the first word go.

Suddenly Pip heard a rough, gritty voice. She was startled when she realized where the other voice was coming from. She saw a beautiful conch shell on the floor of the cave. Just as she started to lift the shell, a huge, white cloud of ink appeared. Pip was scooping underneath the shell, and a slimy tentacle slipped around her arm.

"Just a moment, Tidbit. Just who do you think you are?" The rock continued ejecting white clouds, and a guitar sound revealed the presence of Pedro—a paranoid octopus. He was blasting out Pip's lullaby in a bluesy beat. Spontaneously, he stopped.

Pip urged Pedro to continue. "Sing your favorite tune!"

Pedro shrugged. "What do I possibly have t o sing about? Three quarters of my fans were lost in the last oil spill. The sea creatures are homeless—there's no shelter, and music is dead, so forget about a sea concert."

Pip said, "But you sound awesome! Come on, Pedro. Play a riff, one measly lick for a kid. Go on. You're kickin'!"

Pedro lowered his beady eyes. "OK, just one tune." He picked up his guitar and electrified the ocean with his sound. The music attracted hundreds of fans that had been waiting patiently outside Pedro's sea cave. Pedro and Pip were unaware of their presence. Pedro blasted.

PREACHIN' FUTURE FROM THE PAST

What's the use in trying
After all these years of hiding?
Did I think that I could win?
My voice its too thin.
Yet the child pushes me forward,
Shows me how to spin.
Can I hold my ground firmly?
Using strength against sin,
Will I tumble if they hurt me?
Will I shrink if they desert me?
Has my legend lost its power?
Or am I merely a coward.
Should I seek another answer?
To a question put to rest?

Is there really any wisdom?
Preaching' future from the past.

Pedro began to squeeze Pip because he was exhilarated by his performance. Though Pip tugged to get free, the pressure increased. She wedged her foot between a rock and a clam, but Pedro's tentacle kept pulling.

"Stop it. You're hurting me," screamed Pip.

Pedro said, "Look, you little half pint, I'm no babysitter. You best be on your way? Or I might have to eat you."

Pip told Pedro, "I'm from New Orleans, and I'm here to help you. I can clean up the ocean!"

Pedro's anger subsided. "New Orleans? You aren't a billionaire, are you?" He sulked and let her go. He hadn't sung in years. "Everyone knows I'm washed up."

Pip looked terrified. She started to cry. "I'm lost. I was with Jaime, and he returned to the land without me. I think I want to go home now."

Pedro soothed her. He couldn't stand the sight of crying women. "Now calm down, girlie. You're a real, good singer for a lost child." He told Pip that he was lost once. "I was abandoned. When I was two, my father, a ramblin' man, took off without a word. My momma, who was a beautiful singer, was crushed. She filled the ocean with her tears. She loved my old man more than anyone in the sea. Her heart was so broken that she finally withered away and died. The only thing she left me with was a talent for singing."

With his tentacles, Pedro grabbed a tiny minnow and chomped it down. He said he'd been passed around to several sea caves until he was thirteen, and that was when a tragedy occurred. "*The Suzy Q*, a New Orleans fishing fleet, captured me. The only reason I wasn't made into minced meat was because of my singing. I belted out my favorite song when I was netted, and, instead of killing me, my captors decided to showcase me at the aquarium."

Pip said faintly, "I know where that is."

"Well," Pedro said, "miraculously I escaped by sheer luck. You don't have any cockamamie ideas of capturing me?"

Pip sadly said, "I don't, Pedro. I'm here to help you. Can't you see that? I don't want to capture you. I want to hear you sing. Please. One more."

Pedro thought if Pip's father paid for the cleanup, all the sea creatures could return to work in clean waters. There would be no more homelessness; no more depression; no more disease, and no more despair. It would be worth Pedro's efforts to preach to the creatures, and he would sing again.

Perhaps Pip's appearance was an omen. He frantically called for Consuelo. Pedro whistled, and Juan appeared with two bodyguards.

Suddenly, Jaime fired a dart gun and nearly hit Pedro.

Pedro bellowed, "Juan, what the heck? How did this happen?"

Juan and Consuelo appeared to block Pedro from further harm.

He deposited Pip in front of Juan, who felt somehow responsible for this mistake.

"Oh, master," cried Juan, "We only left you alone for one minute. When they heard your music, the fans went berserk, so we tried to block them from your cave.

Pedro said, "No excuses. What am I?"

Juan meekly said, "A legend." And under his breath he added, "You're nothing, nothing but a fat, old, selfish octopus!"

Pedro ordered Consuelo to remove Pip. Then, he ordered, "Fire these imbeciles and hire some cute starfish as my new bodyguards. "Juan," Pedro spat, "you're now head of wardrobe!"

Not believing what he was hearing, Juan said, "Wardrobe?"

Pedro said, "Dismissed."

Consuelo begged, "Can I have a moment with you, Pedro?" She signaled to Jaime to move Pip from earshot. Jaime rescued Pip and ascended to the top of the sea.

Pip's father was having a conniption fit in the boat. "Cucho," he cried, "call the coast guard! Where the heck is my girl?" Cucho was using the ship-to-shore radio when Jaime resurfaced. There was a lot of confusion on the boat because Pip's father had tripped when he made a frantic attempt to grab the dispatcher and talk to the coast guard himself, and Cucho pushed him overboard by mistake. Cucho said, "Calm down! You're panicking."

Jaime resurfaced with a very tired Pip in his arms. "Help me get Pip onboard!"

Cucho asked, "What happened?"

"Wrong place, wrong time."

Cucho said, "Oh no, not Pedro."

"I think he might have bruised her arm."

Jaime recounted the story about how Pedro was singing and squeezing. He told Cucho how his singing caused a real commotion with the sea creatures because Pedro hadn't sung in years.

Cucho continued to help Pip. "Come to Papa." Just as Pip wrapped her arms around Cucho, her father slopped aboard.

Pip's father took off Pip's gear and said, "Let's have a look at that arm."

Pip murmured, "It's nothing. I'm OK, and the coolest thing happened—I met Pedro." She begged to go scuba diving again. "Pedro is a nice octopus, and he needs help."

Pip's father cut her off, and in confidence said, "Pip, you're very courageous, but these men are thieves. They're robbing us penniless; how about a fishing trip?"

Cucho cut in. "Excuse me, Señor, but we are not thieves. We also do parasailing, fishing, and snorkeling."

Pip cried, "I want to scuba. Dad, please!"

Jaime started up the big white boat, and Cucho steered the wheel toward shore. Pip's father looked at a sulking Pip and held her hand. "Sweetie," he said, "I'll think about it, and you did a superb job."

When they docked the boat, it was nearly six o'clock. Cucho and Jaime said, "Mañana, gringos."

Pip said, "Mañana means 'tomorrow,' right?"

Pip's father said, "Right. Your Spanish is perfect, but I'm broke. We'll try snorkeling mañana."

Cucho and Jaime started singing their sales pitch on another couple waiting at their shack."

After sipping a Shirley Temple and a piña colada, Pip and her father were beat. They ate chicken enchiladas and nachos, and finally they got to their room.

In bed, Pip asked about her father's promise. "Dad, you promised your boss that you would help with the cleanup. We have been learning in science that it all starts with the Gulf."

"What about the Gulf?"

"Because of the oil spill, there is contaminated water and too much silt flowing upriver, choking the cargo lines. The boats can't get where they need to go. Not to mention that the ocean water, which has spilled over the barrier islands, has contaminated the fresh water. The oil spill has put all kinds of fishermen out of business. Did you know we are losing swampland the size of a football fields every day because of global warming?"

"Silt? I didn't realize fourth graders knew this."

Pip said, "I want to be a marine biologist when I grow up because then I can play in the water all day instead of sitting in a dusty office like you."

"Why do you think where I work is bad?"

Pip said, "You're in a grumpy mood after work a lot."

Pip's father reflected. "It's true. I think I need a new line of work."

"Yes, you need a new vocation. If we really clean the ocean, we can create new opportunities for fishermen who are responsible for the gigantic supply of seafood that is delivered to the cities, which depends on the health of the Mississippi. The ocean is the gateway."

Pip's father said, "I know our oil spill really messed up a lot of folks' lives."

Pip was enthusiastic. "OK then, let's do it."

"Where did you learn all this?"

"It's on all the enviro sites!"

"When did you go green?"

"Come on, Dad. You have got to get Pedro help?"

Pip's father said, "But scuba diving is dangerous, and anyway, I'm not a god darn fish. I prefer to give and live on land."

"But, Dad, you said...?"

"Well, I will think about it. We need to go back home and do some research. Get some engineers on board. Now let's get some rest."

"Can we scuba again tomorrow?"

"I'd like to try snorkeling. Look what the octopus did to your arm?"

"But I want to see Pedro again."

Her dad stroked her hair. "Sweetie, your mother is expecting you home in one piece. We have one more day. Let's play it safe!"

Pip had caused a stir underwater. Pedro had called a conference with Consuelo because, although he was sore and angry, he had been thinking about Pip's courage and strength. His tentacle ached from his struggle with Pip.

Consuelo reprimanded Pedro for his behavior. "Pedro, you were very rude. That kid was here to help!" Consuelo was a peacemaker, and she pointed out to Pedro that if he performed for the world—the land and the sea—the earthlings would care. They might educate themselves about the sea floor, and then they would surely respect the wonderful sea inhabitants.

Pedro crossed four of his tentacles over the other four and snorted in an air bubble. "I'll consider it."

Consuelo yodeled, "On time."

Pedro said, "That kid almost cost me my life. What if she were a fisherman? Consuelo, where are my new bodyguards?"

That afternoon, Consuelo advertised auditions for female bodyguards. She posted a sign outside of Juan's nest.

Juan was pleading with Consuelo, while his other two cronies were announcing auditions. "Please, Consuelo," begged Juan, "I promise it will never happen again!"

A bunch of mixed fish appeared as soon as Consuelo screamed, "Bodyguards, looking for female bodyguards." The male eels were offended, and Consuelo said, "Boys, beat it!"

Juan grunted, "Females! Not only have I lost my position, but to chicks."

"Juan! You're so pitiful."

Consuelo directed the aspiring female starfish into Pedro's

quarters. Pedro viewed three that were dancing a little number that Consuelo made up for them to show off their talent.

The cute one counted then off. "Like a five, like a six, like a seven, like a eight." They began to swirl and sing.

I WANNABE A STAR

I wanna be, I wanna be, I wanna be a star
And if it takes a day, or takes ten years
I'll put up with the tar.
And when I shine, I'll be on time, the world will be all mine,
But now I'll be, oh yes, I'll be, I'll be your bodyguard.

We'll march in threes,
you'll pay our fees to shield you from the slime.
We'll block the people with our star steeples,
And never lose our minds.
You're my man and I'm your fan, I want to have the job
now I'll be, oh yes, I'll be, I'll be your bodyguard.

I wanna be the one who shimmers like the sun.
I want you all to swoon and sway under the moon.
I'll be the babe to touch, your fans they won't get much,
My sharp penta curves will make you faint and swerve.

Like I wanna be, like I wanna be, like I wannabe a star.
But now we'll be, oh yes, we'll be,
We'll be your bodyguards.

"Cut," chirped Consuelo. "Well, Pedro?"

He said, "I like the sister with the slender appendages, and the one with the innocent eyes!"

Consuelo explained that Pedro's security was of utmost importance. Under no circumstances could anyone enter the cave without clearance from Consuelo. The girls exited.

Consuelo remarked, "You know, Pedro, it's time you pump up these senseless sea creatures, because nobody cares about our environment. According to Jaime, this kid really wants to clean the ocean...and if you shine this one, we might lose our homes permanently...What are we going to do with millions of homeless creatures?"

Pedro reflected and agreed with Consuelo. "The kid had a purity, and if the water was clean, I could sing again; all the time." He said, "Maybe an appearance at the Ocean Proscenium, provided that there's no press, no pictures, double security, and no announcements!"

Consuelo was elated. She said she would contact Rodriguez, the concert promoter.

Pedro said, "Arrange wheels to Louisiana, and find out where that kid lives."

Consuelo called the starfish bodyguards. "Yo, Romanita, Concheta, we're going on the road. Change of crib. Call Juan, ladies."

The meek starfish said, "OK, anything else?"

Consuelo added, "Pedro's passaporte, pronto!"

Pedro said, "I love you, Consuelo."

Consuelo blushed, "Me too."

Pedro said, "Now leave me alone. I'd like a private moment."

She darted out of the cave. Pedro said to himself, "At last, a reason to live." There was hope. He was tired of this empire of isolation. He considered his opportunity for a comeback on the concert circuit. He picked up his guitar and strummed. Pedro smiled to himself because his old rock 'n' roll self had emerged. He ejected a white cloud and retired for the evening.

Part 111
The Journey & The Rescue

Back in Pedro's quarters under the sea, Consuelo was assembling the group for a long voyage. Juan and the other eels, the starfish bodyguards, Consuelo, and Pedro were ready to depart.

Consuelo said, "Well, Pedro, like hop to! We're ready to ready to roll."

The means of transportation was Wally the Whale. Celebrities on land traveled by limousine while these sea creatures used Wally the Whale as their "limo." Wally was a friendly whale who protected everyone from harm. He carried the creatures under his belly. They were safe with Wally because he was the king of the sea.

Consuelo continued, "Pedro, you're in the middle of his belly. Romanita and Concheta, wrap around Wally's spout, and Juan, you and your cronies are in the back."

Juan protested that he would not be able to see.

"Stop flappin' your gills, and take a seat. I will ride under Wally's chest because my navigating skills are sharp."

Wally chanted, "Fasten your gills. Ah, whoa, whoa, whoa, off we go."

They all started singing and went happily on their way.

AIN'T NO LIMOS IN HEAVEN

There ain't no limos in heaven,
Babe. That's what I hear 'em say.
If you arrive by six or seven
You can travel by the day.
Land's dangerous by eleven,
That's why we swim this way.
There ain't no limos in heaven,
So we're sticking to the bay.

(Consuelo)
Wally, he's the greatest whale,
He'll always make your bail.
And when the fans start throwing rocks
He gives them all a hail

(Starfish)
Consuelo, she's a pilot fish,
She's Pedro's favorite dish.
When the road gets dark and mossy,
She supplies him any wish.

(Chorus)

(Starfish)
We starfish guard our sacred bus,

We put up with the don't and musts.
And safety is our only thought,
We shield ourselves from Pedro's fuss.

(Pedro)
These silly morons can't keep shut
with mundane banter about bad luck.
If we ever reach the land on time
We'll probably all get stuck.

Chorus

(Wally) RAP
I love to be the ocean wheels, for Pedro makes a hefty deal.
Consuelo, she's the toughest mate. She knows just how Pedro feels.
When we get lost I know the shores,
but Pedro, man, can start a war.
I love to migrate on the road, I'm responsible for this load.
(Chorus) (Coda) There. Ain't no limos in Heaven, babe...

Unfortunately, Wally the Whale had lost his direction because the ocean was so murky when they were trying to cross the border into the Louisiana side of the Gulf of Mexico. Navigating became too confusing during the night. Generally, Wally would use the stars as his guides—everyone in the sea knows that if the lights are horizontal, land is approaching—but as it was rainy, there were no lights.

Pedro had drifted from Wally's belly when Wally surfaced. Pedro was totally disoriented. "Hey, Wally! Where are you?"

There was no answer. Consuelo, surfacing with Wally, surveyed the situation. "Another oil spill! We're doomed." She ordered, "Everyone chill!" Suddenly she noticed that Pedro was missing. She panicked.

Pedro had been drifting for over an hour. He muttered, "How, typical. Lost by my own bodyguards...Those idiots...They're all a bunch of lunatics. Where am I?" The sea got calm, and Pedro felt the beach under his belly. He had let the waves roll him in because he knew moving on land would be difficult. When he staggered onto the beach, he reached some sea grass that was moist from the evening dew.

Just as he was pulling his last tentacles into the camouflaging grass, an officer shined a light into his eyes. The officer's eyes widened with shock, and then they showed gleeful surprise. He said, "Excuse me, but aren't you that famous octopus that belongs in our newly renovated aquarium?"

Not thinking, he was speaking in Spanish, he said, "No, gracias!"

Big mistake. The customs officer insisted on seeing his papers and his passport. Lots of Mexicans had been creeping across his station lately, and the officer was not about to get reprimanded for an alien octopus. Pedro stalled for time. He tried ejecting a white cloud but couldn't muster his energy. He stuttered, "Sí, Señor," as he hooked a tentacle around the customs officer's leg.

The customs officer grabbed his tentacle, handcuffed it, and beamed the flashlight back into Pedro's beady eyes. "You are that octopus...the famous singer who escaped two years ago. You're under arrest. I was almost fooled. You appear to be black. You are white though, aren't you?"

Pedro resisted the officer, all eight tentacles gripping him. He spat, "You idiot! I'm black because of the oil spill. You should be under arrest—for murder. There are millions of dead sea creatures because of your human negligence!"

"Belligerent as well!" The customs officer administered Pedro's rights and asked the famous octopus if he'd like a lawyer before he returned him to the aquarium officials.

Pedro, gasping for air, requested Pip. "She's a little girl who's a good singer. Find her."

The customs officer howled with laughter and bragged about how he was going to be a hero. "Wait till the *Gambit* reports on this. I'll make front page." He scooped up Pedro and yelled, "Yeha, Dixie!"

The following afternoon, Pip was watching *The Jetsons*. It was fate when she heard the newscaster announce: "Aquarium officials are happy to reclaim 'Famous Pedro'. The singing octopus was recaptured yesterday while crossing the border."

Pip felt a sudden stab at her heart. Pedro looked sick.

Back in his tank, Pedro started screaming, "Hey, gringo, I'm looking for Pip. Tu tienes agua? This is hardly like the ocean. I need my people. Pip, Consuelo, Wally, help!" Pedro picked up his guitar and blasted out "Homesick."

HOMESICK

Some people forgot to think that they wiped out their link,
And they're wrong, baby, they're wrong.
I go to sleep at night, ignoring my anxious fright,
Wondering why, I left home.

And I dream alone that your face appears near.
I miss you holding my heart and calming my fears.
Well, I'm so broken inside, I find no hope from these lies.
And, I just can't find, goin' out of my mind.

Well, I'm just dust in this world,
rollin' along in a whirl. Nowhere bound, Floundering 'round.
When I open my eyes,
I'm disconnected from time,
And I'm lost, baby, I'm lost.

Maybe one day, I'll look to the bay
And I'll see you headed my way,
That sparklin' glint in your eyes
Your prince like disguise,
And we'll cry, baby, we'll cry.

Oh, I just can't find. Oh, I'm so darn blind.
My world is so unkind.
Going out of my mind, out of my mind,
Out of my mind, out of my mind.

Pip quickly switched off the tube and dashed outside. Her mother was pruning her rose bushes. "Where's my little helper?"

"I don't want to garden, Mom!"

Her mother urged Pip. "If you and I don't take care of the earth, who will?" She tied back the branches to train them along the lattice.

Pip was moody. "Seaweed takes care of the earth when he buries his bones."

Ever since Pip had returned from Mexico, she had been depressed. Pip's mother saw this as an opportunity to inquire about Pip's feelings. "Pip, what happened on the scuba diving trip? Honey, you can tell me?"

She blushed, shrugged, and hugged Seaweed like he was a security blanket. Seaweed drooled all over her hand. Pip said, "I got all excited diving, but Dad wussed out because of a humongous barracuda and went back to the boat. While I was alone, I met some cool eels and starfish and this famous rocktopus named Pedro."

Pip's mother arched an eyebrow. "A rocktopus?"

"Yes. I was feeling so great. I told him Dad could raise the funds to clean up the mess. Pedro got mad, and he said he wasn't for sale."

"Wait a second, he could speak? Pip, I don't know any speaking octopi."

"You don't scuba dive, Mom. Sea creatures can communicate. I thought Pedro was so cool, but I failed him, Mom. I failed!"

Pip's Mom hugged Pip. Seaweed got squashed between mother and daughter and ran away. She was slightly concerned about Pip's imaginary story but, nevertheless, consoled her. "Failure is never fatal and success is never final!" She wiped Pip's tiny tears that began to drop down her cheek. To encourage her daughter, she started gently singing her favorite lullaby.

DON'T QUIT

When things go wrong, as they sometimes will
When the road you're treading, seems all uphill
When the funds are low, and the debts are high
When you want to smile, but you have to sigh
When things are getting you down a bit
Rest if you must, but don't you quit.

Life seems queer with its twists and turns
And many of us often learn
We could have captured the victory cup
Had we fought for a while and not given up
When care is pressing you down a bit
Rest if you must, but don't you quit.

Success is failure, turned inside out
The silver tint on the clouds of doubt
And you never can tell how close you are
It may be near when it seems so far
Stick to the fight when you are hardest hit
And when things go wrong you must not quit
Rest if you must, but don't you quit.

Pip's Mom gave Pip an extra squeeze of confidence. "Remember, dear, it's courage that counts!" Pip hugged her mom. She dumped all her gardening gear in a basket and said, "Be a gem, put this away."

Pip said, "Sure, Mom," and when her mother was out of hearing distance, she said to Seaweed, "I got to get back to Pedro. Come on." Seaweed lifted his ears and followed her lead. "We're going to test your search and rescue skills. Let's go!"

Pip's Mom asked, "Where are you going?"

"Girl Scouts. Bye Mom."

Her mom waved and resumed deadheading her roses, and then she said, "But Pip, Girl Scouts meets tomorrow."

"It's cookie sales, remember, Mom," and then repeated her mother's old saying: "Don't quit, right?"

Her mom winked, and Pip winked back. "That's my girl. Be careful!"

Later that night after her parents were dining in the kitchen, Pip's father buried himself in the *Sentinel*. On the front cover was a picture of a smiling customs officer and Pedro. Her mom had her eye glued to the driveway when she said, "Dear, I'm getting worried. Pip is never this late."

Her father said, "Why are you concerned? You do nothing but worry."

It was true—Pip's mom was a worrywart, though Pip always returned home before dark. On second thought, Pip's story that she was attending a special cookie sales meeting at the Girl Scouts was absurd. Mom was trying to get Pip's father's attention when she noticed the headlines and tore the paper out of his hands.

He said, "Since when do you read the news?"

She was speechless. She kept pointing to the octopus, too filled with fear. She said, "Pip doesn't have Girl Scouts today."

Pip's father finished her thought by saying, "You don't think…"

And she finally said, "Absolutely!" He told her to wait at home, and he would go to the aquarium and personally pick her up. The last thing he needed was more press after the oil spill.

Her mom fearfully blurted, "Hurry, dear. Even a blind pig will find an acorn sometimes."

Pedro was in a large aquarium with lots of algae eaters and shells on the bottom. He was muttering to himself, "This whole mission's a bust. I've been tricked into this suction-squeezing mess." Just then, he saw Pip.

Pip dipped her hand in the water and got the salty smell of Pedro on a napkin. She waved it under her pup's nose, giving Seaweed the scent of his rescue. Once Seaweed got the gamey command, Pip meekly asked the guard, "Is this Pedro?"

The guard, an old, Irish man with a curly mustache said, "Why yes, lassie. You can have a look at him, but just for a few minutes; we close at eight."

Pip made a stop sign to Seaweed and commanded him to the tank.

Pip summoned all of her courage and distracted the

guard. "Can you show me where another bathroom is? I tried the one over here, but the door was locked?"

The guard, relieved of his post, said, "Of course, deary." As he led the way, Seaweed got to work.

Seaweed approached the aquarium tank, took a leap, landed in the water, and swam to Pedro. Pedro threw a tentacle around his neck. Pedro said, "I've never trusted a dog before, but here it goes. Get me to water as quickly as possible. Can you do that?"

Seaweed nodded.

"OK...Now, careful. Watch my tentacles, careful of my suction cups, go a little to your right...that's it!"

Pedro thought of Consuelo, which reminded him why he was in this situation in the first place. The thought of Consuelo trying to make peace among the sea creatures moved Pedro to tears.

Pip came running in without the guard. "Quick, Seaweed. Follow me!"

Pedro asked. "where's your old man? We're going to improve our world, you with me, right? If your dad can raise the capital to clean the ocean, I'll sing on Ocean Day. It will end the doom that has descended to the depths of the sea. It's Pedro 'n' Pip!"

Pip said, "You got it." She moved Pedro safely out of Seaweed's clutches and exited the aquarium. Once on the street, Pedro started strumming a rap.

PEDRO 'N' PIP'S RAP
(PIP)
Something's taken hold of our population,
Destroying our homes and our generation.
Waste material across our nation,
Leaks causing disintegration.
Check out this oil situation
Oil and trash in concentrations.

(Pedro)
Pedro is the name by which I go,
Playin' guitar is something I know.
In a concert at sea, I can cause a splash

To help clear up this toxic clash.
Pip, my friend, has the same plan too,
She can help me here, there's something to do.
But don't you cross me or I'll get mean,
We're the kings and the queens of the underwater scene.

(Pip)
Pip's my name, I'm ten years old,
Swimming and scuba is something I know,
Living on land I can raise the funds,
My father's the ticket, that's the one.
Pedro mi amigo, we have the same plan,
We'll spread the word 'cause that's our reign.
But don't you worry I'll make the team,
We're the kings and queens of the underwater scene.

(Pedro)
Pedro 'n' Pip, were a team
Don't you cross us, or we'll get mean
Relax, be cool, and keep life clean
We're the kings and the queens of the underwater scene.

(PIP & Pedro)
Something's taken hold of our population,
Destroying our homes and our generation.
Waste material across our nation.
Leaks causing disintegration.
Check out this water situation:
Oil and trash in concentrations.

(Pedro)
Pedro 'n' Pip, were a team
Don't you cross us, or we'll get mean
Relax, be cool, and keep life clean
We're the kings and the queens of the underwater scene...

Pip, Pedro, and Seaweed skipped down the sidewalk, and the streetlights led them home. Pedro hung on Pip's waist.

Meanwhile Pip's dad entered the museum and asked the guard, "Excuse me, but have you seen a little girl who is yay high?"

The Irish guard, who was known to be forgetful said, "No, and it's closing time."

Just at that moment, the guard discovered Pedro's empty aquarium. He screamed, "Pedro, where is Pedro?"

Pip's father quickly left. On the sidewalk, he pulled out his cell phone and called his wife.

She was desperate when the phone rang. She was pacing back and forth in the kitchen. She ran to the phone, and while answering it, Pip quietly entered the kitchen through the back door.

Pedro was under Pip's Girl Scouts troop banner. His head created a large bulge in Pip's stomach. Pedro was whispering, "Hurry before she spots me." Pip waltzed by her mother, who had her back turned to her.

Her mother turned around at the sound of their voices, and Pip made it swiftly to her room.

"Pip," her mother wailed, "where have you been?"

She said, "I told you. I was selling the cookies."

"That's a lie," she said.

She described to her mother how she had been selling cookies with her friend, and her friend's mother asked her if they wanted to get pizza, so she said yes, and that was why she was late. Pip quickly added, "I ate too much of those tasty taga-longs, and I think I'm going to get sick."

Pip's mother said, "Well, I don't believe that you're telling the whole truth. Your father went to the aquarium looking for you. Do you know anything about that?"

Pip closed the door to her bedroom. "No Mom. Just a second, I need to use the bathroom."

Her mother was suspicious. "We will deal with this when your father gets home."

Impatient, Pip's father was screaming on the telephone, "What's going on?"

Her mom dashed to the phone. "Sorry to leave you hanging, dear, but Pip just got home, and she's acting strange. You ground her. She's your daughter!"

When her father got home, Pip was punished for lying about her whereabouts. Her parents went to bed angry. Pip felt terrible for lying, but she had made a promise to Pedro that she intended to keep. They were a team, though their team was fading because Pedro was drying up. Pip was lying in bed, gazing out the window at the stars, when Pedro whimpered, "Yo, Pip. ¿Tu tienes agua?" Pedro was resting in the salad bowl her mother had brought her in case she threw up.

Pip said, "Agua, oh, 'water,' right", I've got a bowl right here beside my bed."

Pedro, said, "I need salty water and more space."

Pip was worried. "Give me some time; I am trying to come up with a solution."

"Madre de Dios, think of something." Pedro started tapping Pip's head. Her father's snoring, which sounded like a monotonous saw, interrupted their thoughts. "The bathtub," whispered Pip. "With all that noise, they'll never hear us!" Pip scooped up Pedro and silently crept down the hallway. When they entered the bathroom, Pip bumped into the sink and hurt one of Pedro's tentacles.

"Ouch!" Pedro cried.

Pip agonized and promised she would try to be more careful, but if they switched on a light, her mom might awaken. She turned on the water in the sink and rested Pedro there for a few moments.

Pedro was hardly quenched by the sink water. It wasn't the same as the ocean. "Hey," he said, "you wouldn't happen to have any salt around?"

Pip said, "Not sea salt, but Morton Salt. It's downstairs in the kitchen."

Pedro said, "Get it."

Pip dashed out the door. Pedro heard her knock into a box or something, but it only increased the volume of Pip's father's snoring.

She returned with the whole container and dumped it into the running tub water. It was nice and warm. "OK, Pedro, I'm going to transfer you."

Pedro suggested, "Do it carefully. I'm hurt." Once in the tub, Pip sprinkled salt all over Pedro.

He cried, "Watch it! It's stinging my eyes."

Pip, beginning to feel overwhelmed, started giving Pedro encouragement by stroking his eyes. "I'm sorry, Pedro. I guess it's not the same as sea salt, Morton Salt hurts my eyes too."

Pedro started to cry. He explained that he always wanted to see what living on land was like, but it seemed impossible for him to survive in Pip's environment. Pip started crying too. Pip said she loved scuba diving, but she couldn't survive in the ocean.

"I know. You need air, but Pip, the sea creatures are counting on you. They want rock 'n' roll, and, even more, then they want a clean sea. Without your help, everyone will die. Ocean Day is tomorrow; we have to go to Mexico, you understand?" Pedro extended his eight tentacles. He plugged the tips of them all around the tub.

Pip could see that Pedro was desperate. She assured him that things always worked themselves out, and that she promised to help. "My father can help, just you wait!" Pedro nudged her. Pip kissed him, and said, "I have to get to sleep. I am so tired; the water is shriveling up my fingers. Look."

Pedro knew that he himself would not last through the next day, unless he reached the sea. He had lost his strength.

EVERYBODY KNOWS

Everybody knows we're going down
When we walk around.
Everybody knows we're going down
When we're out on the town.
I pray each day,
I won't be betrayed.
Everybody knows there is an end,
Can't avoid the trend.
Everybody knows there is an end
That you can't defend.
I pray each day
I won't be betrayed.
The river runs free of chains.

The sea keeps the waves company.
The trees will drop all their leaves
On the hills eternally.
I pray each day,
I won't be betrayed
Everybody knows we're going down.

"Pedro, Pedro you have to hang in there for me one more day...I'm going to save you. What if we establish a contest for Ocean day?"

"What about the fish that are dying now like me?"

Pip stammered. "I don't know how to save them. But I can save you.

Pedro had learned a wonderful lesson from Pip. When they met, Pedro was scared of human beings. When he was younger, humans had been cruel to him, and he had been filled with rage and the desire for revenge from the time he had first escaped from the aquarium. But Pip was a different kind of human. She offered protection, advice, and rescue. Pedro felt relieved when Pip was around. He felt safe with her. Pip had taught him forgiveness. She taught him that not everyone on land was greedy and selfish.

Pedro let down his guard and dozed knowing that there was hope with a team like Pedro 'n' Pip.

Pip lay on the bath mat. She dozed, holding one of Pedro's tentacles.

The next morning, her father was banging on the bathroom door. "Pip, open the door?"

Pip, still holding a frozen tentacle, nudged Pedro. There was no response. Her father continued calling her name, while she tried to revive the octopus.

He was knocking loudly. "Pip! I'd like a word with you."

"Coming, Dad!"

Pedro lifted a helpless, weary eyelid and told Pip he was nearly finished. Pip gently rubbed his face and assured Pedro that he was OK, and most importantly that it's Ocean Day.

Her father burst into the bathroom and said, "Sweetheart, answer me." He was startled when he saw Pedro in the tub. "What the heck? Pedro? I suspected as much."

Pedro lifted a tentacle and wrapped it around Pip's father's neck. Her father's face started turning red.

Pip said, "Pedro! Stop it! Dad can help us."

Pedro let go reluctantly. His eight tentacles shriveled into a tiny ball. He had spots on his belly and was the size of an ice cream bowl. He nudged Pip.

Pip meekly acknowledged to her father that Pedro was stolen from the aquarium. She protested, "Pedro was really lost, and I promised him I'd save his life. And we have very little time to do that. What about our deal? You said you would raise the cash to clean up the oil spill that spread to Mexico."

Pip's father agonized with Pip, trying to come up with a solution. "I'm out of cash, Pip. Saxton Oil cut my wages, and we're still recovering from the monetary losses of the oil spill. I simply don't have the money."

Suddenly Pedro's eyes widened with seething anger. "Busted! Did you say Saxton?"

Pip's father said, "Why yes, what's it to you, you little appetizer?"

Pedro tightened his hold on Pip's father with each question. "Does Saxton have a receding hairline? Is he a pompous porker who smokes cigars?" Pip's father nodded meekly.

"Does he own a fishing boat called the *Greedy Gal*?"

"Why yes, I've fished on the boat several times. He loves that boat more than he loves his family."

Pedro reminded Pip about the story he had told him about being captured by the fishing fleet that initially put him behind bars at the aquarium. Pip assured Pedro she understood. "Same gringo."

Pip's father was getting anxious. "Pip, don't you think we should turn Pedro in to the aquarium officials?"

For the first time in her life, Pip stood her ground. She said, "Positively no!"

Pedro was defiant. "I thought you were on our side!"

Suddenly, Pip's mother's voice was booming in the hallway. She was ranting about the *Gambit* headlines: 'Famous Octopus Stolen'. She said it described a young girl fleeing from the aquarium with the creature under her shirt. The description fit Pip.

Pip's father dismissed his wife's accusation. "Don't be ridiculous, woman. Pip is with me." He suddenly recognized his daughter's courage. "This means everything to you, doesn't it?"

Pip said, "Yes, Dad. What's more important than rock 'n' roll?"

"I'm so proud of you! You've got the guts to stand up for your own beliefs." He smiled at Pip and shook her hand. "Pip, my girl, I believe you have a deal. Saving Pedro is our only mission."

Pedro loosened his grip and smiled slyly at Pip's father. "That's my man."

Pip's father opened the door and said, "Honey, I'm shaving. Put breakfast on the table. Pip and I have an outing planned." He then closed the door and asked Pedro what to do.

The thought of Saxton infuriated Pedro. He said, "Take me to Saxton, I'll take it from there."

Pip was with Pedro. She pushed her father in the direction of the kitchen and said, "Move it, Dad." Pip wrapped Pedro around her chest.

Pedro said, "Wait, get your iPhone. It will be useful."

Pip did, and when they passed through the kitchen, her father put his hand over her mother's mouth and signaled, "No questions." Her eyes bulged, and they both blew her a kiss. They ran out the door with Pedro screaming, "I'll destroy your empire, Morty Saxton."

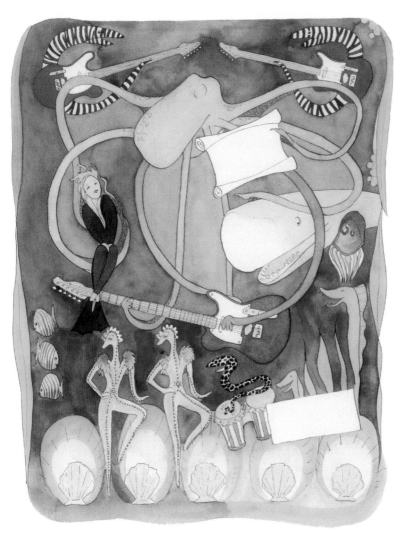

Part 1V
Ocean Day

As they entered the tall, office building belonging to Saxton Oil, Pip's father walked with great confidence. He nodded to the security guard. "Looking good, Joe!" He held Pip's hand and Pip held Pedro securely under her shirt.

On the way up the elevator, Pedro was fascinated with the elevating feeling. He commented to Pip on the sensation. "I feel like I'm ascending in the ocean."

"Yes, it does feel a little like that, doesn't it?" Pip said that maybe the human condition was similar to that of the underwater world. "We just need air."

Pedro changed the subject. "Wait till he sees me; he'll have a coronary."

Pip's father said, "Pedro, be quiet until we are in Morty's quarters."

Even though Pedro was riding on his last burst of energy, it was a fight he would not miss. Saxton had tried to take his life. Now he would have an opportunity to punish Saxton for his cruelty to sea creatures.

Pip's Dad burst through the office door. Mary was seated outside Morty's office suite.

"I've got to see Morty."

Mary, confused by Pip's father's abruptness said, "You will have to wait!"

"Mary, I'm sorry, but this is urgent!"

Meanwhile, Pedro and Pip had crept around Mary's desk and caught a glimpse of Morty. Pedro said, "Look at him, a conniving, smug, fat thief. Turn on your video."

Pip turned on the camcorder on her iPhone.

Morty was seated in a big, leather chair with his feet on the desk. He was smoking a huge Robusto cigar and talking into a speakerphone. "That's right, Zack. Brilliant recovery. But I'm no fool...I stashed three million in my son's trust fund...My seven-year-old wears the pants around here." He paused when he heard the disturbance outside his office, the argument between Mary and Pip's father.

Mary raised her voice one decibel. "He's taking no appointments."

"Mary," bellowed Pip's father, "he's going to see me!"

Pedro and Pip ducked when Morty screamed, "Hey, cut out that racket."

"I'm conducting business here!" He then turned in his chair and continued talking as he looked out his window. "I've got my sights on retiring and turning the Greedy Gal into a commercial fishing line. I'll run trips to Mexico and back. I'll be racking in the dough."

Pedro laughed and said, "Illegal operations out of the States."

Pip held up the recorded video and turned it off. Pip said,

"We got him red-handed. Now what?"

"Pip, the fun has just begun. Hey, that's a good rhyme."

Pip's father scooped Pedro up, and Pip ran in front of him. They all said together, "We're coming in!"

Mary tried to stop them. "But we're in a state of emergency!"

Pedro jumped up on a huge oil barrel that served as a decorative piece beside Morty's desk. He extended his tentacles to Morty's mouth and sang.

EIGHT-CHORD STAR (REPRISE)
I'm a rock 'n' roll octopus,
I'm big, I'm huge, I'm fabulous! A rock 'n' roll octopus,
An eight-chord star, don't make a fuss.

"What is this?" demanded Morty.

Pedro said, "A coup, boss. You're going on a permanent vacation."

Pedro threatened him with an ink cloud, and Morty was so disoriented he fell off his chair.

Pip's father instructed Morty to request his Learjet immediately. Secondly, he produced a contract that stated Morty was personally contributing twenty million dollars to Sea-Help. Pedro assisted Morty with his checkbook, which was conveniently located in the inside pocket of his jacket. Pip's father's last order was for Morty to sign his resignation papers, which also appointed Pip's father as president of Saxon Oil.

Pedro said, "Morty, you are history, bro." Pedro showed his poisonous teeth and said, "Sign!" Pedro told Pip he felt like a king, and then he said, "Isn't Morty a first-rate wimp?"

Pip's father added, "Morty, you are a fat, hairy, smelly scum of a boss. Always, blaming your employees for your mistakes!"

Pip mimicked Pedro and said, "You reap what you sow, mister!"

Morty reluctantly signed everything, and Pedro told Pip to bring him to the jet. He then jumped on Morty's back and ordered Morty to give Mary the contract.

Pip's father added, "Tell her to notify the press of your resignation." Pip's father thanked Pedro for the job promotion.

"De nada," said Pedro.

Pip said, "Let's go, we're out of time. Pedro is dying."

Mary looked entirely terrified when they approached her desk. Pedro got into Morty's face until Morty barely whispered, "Mary, Mr. Sampson will now be the official president of Saxton Oil."

Bewildered, Mary said, "Sir, there's a police commissioner who's in our lobby, some business about some scandal with the captain of the barge. Uh, will I be seeing you in the future?"

Morty said, "No."

Pip said, "So long, Morty."

Pip's father said, "As the new president, Mary, I'm giving you a promotion. You're now my assistant." Pip, smiled. Pedro howled.

She mused. "Well, thank you, Mr. Sampson."

Pedro wrapped a cozy, tentacle around Mary and gave her a tight squeeze. "Girlfriend, take the rest of the day off."

"Mary, my daughter and I will be scuba diving for the rest of the weekend. Call an employee meeting for Monday morning."

Mary winked, and Pedro said, "Adiós, señorita."

Morty looked mortified, and Pedro said, "I hope the food's not fish in prison...might give you heartburn and the runs, especially if it's calamari from the Gulf!"

They carried Pedro in an oil barrel from Morty's office that was filled with salty water onto the Learjet. Pedro was barely breathing after the episode, but Pip held out hope. Pip's father chatted with the pilot about his promotion. "Can you imagine? Morty was intentionally planning an illegal fishing operation. My daughter Pip caught it on tape...on her iPhone. What a crook!" The rest of the trip was spent anticipating Mexico. They would have to smuggle Pedro through customs.

They arrived in Mexico in the afternoon. The sun was very hot. Pip's father rolled the barrel up to the customs officer. Pip prayed for a miracle. And sure enough, an angel appeared in the form of Jaime. He was dressed as an officer now, and he didn't recognize them. He said, "Papers, turistas, por favor?"

Pedro, barely audible, said, "Hurry up, gringo. We've got two hours until Ocean Day."

Pip blurted out, "Jaime, what are you doing here?" Jaime recognized Pip and explained that in Mexico, it is best to be a jack-of-all-trades. In fact, he had several jobs.

Pip told Jaime that they were in desperate need of his help. His father's cell phone rang. It was Mary. She confirmed Pip's father's suspicions.

"Really?" Pip's father arched his eyebrow while listening intently. "Pip," he said. "The captain admitted that Saxton paid him off to collide with the other tanker." Instead of raising cash for the cleanup, Morty was running an insurance scam. And his little boy confided during show-and-tell that he was a millionaire. But the best part was that Morty went to the bank to stop payment on the check to SEA-HELP but it had already cleared.

Pip high-fived her Dad. "AWESOME!"

Her father said, "Our mission has just begun. We'll see to it that the funds are distributed!"

Jaime appeared reluctant to help Pip. He was asking his routine questions: "Anything to declare-animales, dólares, señor? One hundred dólares, no questions, we don't open bags."

Pip's father paid him off. Pedro grabbed the money and shoved it back in Pip's father's pocket. He ordered Jaime to get him to water...pronto. Pedro squirted his last ink cloud to block the view of the other guard officials.

Jaime, petrified, said, "OK, Señor Pedro, anything you want." They all passed through the gates. Pip rolled the barrel out to the curb. Cucho was waiting, dressed in civilian clothes with a sign in front of his cab that read Cucho's Taxi. Jaime mouthed, "It's Pedro." Cucho, terrified, ushered everyone into the cab.

Pip said, "Wicked!"

By the time they reached the beach, it was dusk. All the tourists were hanging around the pool drinking mojitas. Jaime ran ahead of everyone and switched into his wet suit. Cucho followed and hung a sign in front of the shack that read "abierto," which means, "open." Pip approached the shack, and they broke out in their old sales pitch.

> *PASSAPORTE REQUIRED (REPRISE)*
> *By the cabana, we offer three rules:*
> *You pay us first,*
> *Don't get sun burned,*
> *Passaporte required*

Pip played along, "Yo, Jaime, Yo, Cucho: scuba?"

Jaime said, "Waterski?"

Cucho said, "Parasail, jet ski," and then both men said, "Oh no, not them!"

Pip's father laughed and said, "Never say never...Or, as my 1wife would say, 'I'm not impressed by what you say, only what you do!'"

Jaime hung the "Cerrado" sign, and mouthed, "closed." Pip thought that the two thieves were hilarious. They all piled into the boat, suited up for scuba, and went out to sea. They tooted the little horn as they left the harbor. Pip carefully extracted Pedro from the barrel and kissed his head. Pedro spotted Consuelo. He started singing to her.

> *MOVE ME*
> *(Pedro)*
> *You touch my core with one of your chords,*
> *I reach out, but you're gone.*
>
> *(Consuelo)*
> *You reach for me, but I've gone to the sea,*

You say soon I'll be home.

(Pedro)
Well, I'll move you, and you'll move me,
And we'll keep on moving until we can be.
I'll move you, and you'll move me, and
We'll keep on moving until we're released free.

(Pedro)
You tilt that seasaw
I go flying
I think that I'm dying

(Consuelo)
Those joyous angels say that flying
Well, I'm nearly crying

(Consuelo and Pedro)
oh baby, I'll move you, and you'll move me
And we'll keep on moving until we can be.
I'll move you and you'll move me, and we'll
Keep on moving, until we're released free.

Pedro and Consuelo started descending toward Pedro's quarters. Pip and Jaime jumped overboard, and Cucho and her dad followed. Juan's eels were acting as guides.

Juan was at the head, and, as usual, they were all tangled up. "Follow me. Right this way!"

Pedro and Consuelo were now hugging in his quarters. He was so happy to see Consuelo, and he proposed to her by singing. Bells accompanied the song.

(Pedro)
You draw the curtain,
Rip off the bedspread,
Ooh, we're gonna be wed.

(Consuelo)
I kiss your lashes.

(Pedro)

You stroke my belly.

(Consuelo)
Oooh, it feels like jelly.

(Consuelo and Pedro)
Well, I'll move you, and you'll move me
And we'll keep on moving until we can be.
I'll move you and you'll move me, and we'll
Keep on moving until we're released free, move me.
Oh, baby, I'll move you, and you'll move me, and
We'll keep on moving until we can be.
I'll move you, and you'll move me, and we'll keep on moving
Until we're released free, move me, just be, free.

Pedro and Consuelo vowed never to leave each other again. "Till death do we part," whispered Consuelo. Then she urged Pedro to hurry up. The concert was scheduled to begin in thirty minutes. Pedro commented on his ability to be prompt. "On time," wailed Consuelo.

Meanwhile, Pip had been ushered into the ocean concert hall. There was lots of dancing in a huge ballroom. The fish were filled with excitement. There were fans hailing her. She had no idea she was a celebrity. The stage was set up for the program at the front of the room. Juan was playing drums, and the other two eels played bass and electric guitar. The eels took their positions. The two starfish were featured on the side as back-up singers. The fish began waving their gills, chanting "Pedro 'n' Pip, Pedro 'n' Pip." Pip went backstage to meet Pedro.

Pedro wrapped all eight tentacles around Pip. He said, "Gracias, Pip. You mean the world to me. I'm going to miss you."

Pip patted him on the head and said, "Me too. Know that you will always be safe, especially on land."

Pedro assured Pip that she would always be safe in the

sea. She was the sea creatures' hero. He cried a tear and admitted that he loved Pip.

"I love you so, too, Pedro. Even though we will always be separated from time to time, I'll always come back to visit."

"We're a wonderful team."

Pip assisted Pedro with his guitar and sat on a stool off a coral stage. Consuelo introduced Pedro: "Yo, people, I'm proud to announce the King is here. Pedro is home." The sea creatures stopped dancing. Pedro staggered on stage, and the joyous sea creatures started clapping. Wally the Whale was making loud noises that sounded like pipes creaking. He was serving as the bodyguard on stage.

Pedro gave an opening speech. "Thank you. I mean, gracias. I've been around the world, and I'm happy to say that I've made a very large step toward achieving peace with the landlubbers. In fact, some of them will be joining me shortly. The good news is we're going to have our homes back. Every effort will be made to maintain our sea. And now I'm happy to introduce Pip, our guide on land."

Pip shyly said, "Uh, hi, folks…um…that's my dad; and that's Jaime and Cucho, and we're here to help. No more fear of being caught." Her father, Jaime, and Cucho were next to Wally the Whale.

The sea creatures began to cheer.

"Thank you. My father has promised to establish an oceanographic fund. This fund will provide for several thousand workers to clean not only the waters but also all the animals that were hurt by the oil spill. We'll be removing all the toxic waste from the sea. Thank you very much, and now—Pedro."

Juan started drumming, the other two eels joined in, and Pedro strummed his guitar. He sang a number called "Eight-Chord Star."

EIGHT-CHORD STAR

If you live out loud, you attract a crowd
But you pay a heavy toll.
These enchanting faces, in unusual places
It's the world of rock 'n' roll.

When the lights come down, and they settle down
The cries echo master.
When the band begins, by my menacing grin,
My joyous heart beats faster.

(Chorus)

Well, I'm a rock 'n' roll octopus,
I'm big, I'm huge,
I'm fabulous
A rock 'n' roll octopus
An eight-chord star,
Don't make a fuss.

I live for fans underwater or on land to sway by my música.
I pick the stylish babes who dress in jade for after gig fiestas.
But when the light appears, I move to
Different spheres,
to play a new venue
And the cheers are wild,
I'm hardly mild,
my soul feels all renewed

(Chorus)

This electrifying machine, serves as my smoke screen
Disguised as a wizard, but I'm really just a nerd
My music makes me king, and my fans they like to sing,
But I'm a meek man, and outcast on the land.

When Pip returned home, her parents were the happiest they had been in years. Pip received ten trips to scuba-dive in Mexico for her Christmas present. Her father was a well-respected oil executive. And her mom was quoted in the *Sentinel* as saying, "Rest if you must, but don't you quit!" They raised an additional ten million dollars for Sea-Help at a charity ball.

Every night Pip fell asleep peacefully and heard Pedro singing while she was dreaming.

THE END.

Please donate generously to www.edf.org
Through their hard efforts, we are a cleaner world.